the everyman series

being God's man...
by resisting the world

Real Men. Real Life. Powerful Truth.

Stephen Arterburn

Kenny Luck & Todd Wendorff

WATERBROOK
PRESS

BEING GOD'S MAN...BY RESISTING THE WORLD
PUBLISHED BY WATERBROOK PRESS
12265 Oracle Boulevard, Suite 200
Colorado Springs, Colorado 80921

ISBN 978-1-57856-915-1

Published in association with the literary agency of Alive Communications, Inc., 7680 Goddard Street, Suite 200, Colorado Springs, CO 80920.

Published in the United States by WaterBrook Multnomah, an imprint of the Crown Publishing Group, a division of Random House Inc., New York.

WATERBROOK and its deer colophon are registered trademarks of Random House Inc.

Printed in the United States of America
2012

10 9 8 7 6 5 4 3

contents

welcome to the every man
Bible study series

As Christian men, we crave true-to-life, honest, and revealing Bible study curricula that will equip us for the battles that rage in our lives. We are looking for resources that will get us into our Bibles in the context of mutually accountable relationships with other men. But like superheroes who wear masks and work hard to conceal their true identities, most of us find ourselves isolated and working alone on the major issues we face. Many of us present a carefully designed public self while hiding our private self from view. This is not God's plan for us.

Let's face it. We all have trouble being honest with ourselves, particularly in front of other men.

As developers of a men's ministry, we believe that many of the problems among Christian men today are direct consequences of an inability to practice biblical openness—being honest about our struggles, questions, and temptations—and to connect with one another. Our external lives may be in order, but storms of unprocessed conflict, loss, and fear are eroding our resolve to maintain integrity. Sadly, hurting Christian men are flocking to unhealthy avenues of relief instead of turning to God's Word and to one another.

We believe the solution to this problem lies in creating opportunities for meaningful relationships among men. That's why we designed this Bible study series to be thoroughly interactive. When a man practices biblical openness with other men, he moves from secrecy to candor, from isolation to connection, and from pretense to authenticity.

Kenny and Todd developed the study sessions at Saddleback Church in Lake Forest, California, and at King's Harbor Church in Redondo Beach, California, where they teach men's Bible studies. At these studies men hear an outline of the Bible passage, read the verses together, and then answer a group discussion question at their small-group tables. The teaching pastor then facilitates further discussion within the larger group.

This approach is a huge success for many reasons, but the key is that, deep down, men really do want close friendships with other guys. We don't enjoy living on the barren islands of our own secret struggles. However, many men choose to process life, relationships, and pressures individually because they fear the vulnerability required in small-group gatherings. *Suppose someone sees behind my carefully constructed image? Suppose I encounter rejection after revealing one of my worst sins?* Men willingly take risks in business and the stock market, sports and recreation, but we do not easily risk our inner lives.

Many church ministries are now helping men win this battle, providing them with opportunities to experience Christian male companionship centered in God's Word. This study series aims to supplement and expand that good work around the country. If these lessons successfully reach you, then they will also reach every relationship and domain that you influence. That is our heartfelt prayer for every man in your group.

how to use this study guide

As you prepare for each session, first review the **Key Verse** and **Goals for Growth,** which reveal the focus of the study at hand. Discuss as a group whether or not you will commit to memorizing the Key Verse for each session. The **Head Start** section then explains why these goals are necessary and worthwhile. Each member of your small group should complete the **Connect with the Word** section *before* the small-group sessions. Consider this section to be your personal Bible study for the week. This will ensure that everyone has spent some time interacting with the biblical texts for that session and is prepared to share responses and personal applications. (You may want to mark or highlight any questions that were difficult or particularly meaningful so you can focus on those during the group discussion.)

When you gather in your small group, you'll begin by reading aloud the **Head Start** section to remind everyone of the focus for the current session. The leader will then invite the group to share any questions, concerns, insights, or comments arising from their personal Bible study during the past week. If your group is large, consider breaking into subgroups of three or four people (no more than six) at this time.

Next, get into **Connect with the Group,** starting with the **Group Opener.** These openers are designed to get at the heart of each week's lesson. They focus on how the men in your group relate to the passage and topic you are about to discuss. The group leader will read aloud the opener for that week's session and then facilitate interaction on the **Discussion Questions** that follow. (Remember: Not everyone has to offer an answer for every question.)

Leave time after your discussion to complete the **Standing Strong** exercises, which challenge each man to consider, *What's my next move?* As you openly express your thoughts to the group, you'll be able to hold one another accountable to reach for your goals.

Finally, close in **prayer,** either in your subgroups or in the larger group. You may want to use this time to reflect on and respond to what God has done in your group during the session. Also invite group members to share their personal joys and concerns, and use this as "grist" for your prayer time together.

By way of review, each lesson is divided into the following sections:

To be read or completed *before* the small-group session:
- **Key Verse**
- **Goals for Growth**
- **Head Start**
- **Connect with the Word** (home Bible study: 30-40 minutes)

To be completed *during* the small-group session:
- Read aloud the **Head Start** section (5 minutes)
- Discuss personal reaction to **Connect with the Word** (10 minutes)
- **Connect with the Group** (includes the **Group Opener** and discussion of the heart of the lesson: 30-40 minutes)
- **Standing Strong** (includes having one person pray for the group; challenges each man to take action: 20 minutes)

spiritual anthrax: why God's man must not blend with the world

If you think God's values and the world's values can coexist, then think again. Every week as I (Kenny) counsel men, I'm painfully aware of the war of mind and body and spirit raging between the two. Sometimes I feel as though I'm taking an unreasonable stand. But then I recall the words of Scripture: "Do not love the world or anything in the world" (1 John 2:15). To the apostle John, "the world" represented those pursuits and values that could not possibly coexist with his faith. He was simply following Jesus's lead.

Before His death, Jesus gathered His disciples and proclaimed, "If you belonged to the world, it would love you as its own. As it is, you do not belong to the world, but I have chosen you out of the world. That is why the world hates you" (John 15:19). His message to those early disciples still calls to us today: Blending with the world is not the way to follow Jesus.

The good news is that when men get serious about their walk

with God, they feel a deep, intuitive conflict in their souls as they realize that the unholy alliances with the world they once accepted must now be broken. It's a Spirit-induced realization that they've been mixing cocktails of spirituality and worldliness that only produce hangovers of the soul. They start feeling the tension of spiritual warfare, some for the very first time in their lives. And as the battle lines of identity and values become more clearly defined, God's man must choose between God and the world.

The world cherishes image over substance, comfort over character, indulgence over ethics. It confuses net worth with self-worth. It values things over people. And all of these whacked-out priorities pollute our relationship with God and with people.

The apostle James pulled no punches either when he wrote, "Religion that God our Father accepts as pure and faultless is this: ...to keep oneself from being polluted by the world" (James 1:27). Naturally, you wouldn't willingly expose yourself to a deadly poison, such as anthrax. But would you let yourself be overcome by hedonism? Would you breathe in the fumes of narcissism or grab a handful of materialism—and expect to suffer no ill effects? Such things poison a growing relationship with God.

Yes, the world offers its own set of values that can sicken our faith. Yet we can replace these values with the values of Jesus—life-nurturing traits that Jesus looks for in His followers. Men who are able to live out these changes of heart, purpose, and lifestyle will be blessed or will, literally, "live large." (*Note:* The word *blessed* comes from the Greek word *makarios*. The root of this word, *mak*, means "large, lengthy, fortunate." Thus, our use of the phrase "living large" spiritually.)

Developing Christlike values accomplishes two things in God's man. First, it places him in direct opposition to the world's values. In fact, serious training in these values is God's plan for enabling us to overcome the world's influences in our lives. And as we will see, when we seek to live out these values, it will likely generate opposition from others (which is the clearest indicator of progress in becoming God's man).

Second, and more significant, the man who seeks to understand and train in these values will connect more deeply with God. In just ten verses in the book of Matthew, Jesus took religion by the neck and gave the silver boot to the idea that knowing God is about what you do. (See Matthew 5:1-11.) That's the world's way. Instead, Jesus took common religious thinking and flipped it on its head in an awesome sermon, the Sermon on the Mount.

In this study we will focus on the first section of that message, the Beatitudes, in which Jesus described the type of person God blesses. In no uncertain terms, Jesus is saying, "Forget what you thought you knew about loving God. Focus on these traits and live large spiritually."

We intend to do just that in this study. Our goal is to stimulate personal reflection and honest dialogue with God and other men as we focus on Christ's inspired words. As you work through each session, look in the mirror at your own life and ask yourself some hard questions. Whether you are doing this study individually or in a group, realize that complete honesty with yourself, with God, and with others will produce the best results.

Our prayer is that you will engage in battle to be God's man in the ways presented in this study. And that you will stop blending with the world—for good.

don't think your act is together

God's Man Recognizes He Is Helpless Without God

Key Verse

Blessed are the poor in spirit, for theirs is the kingdom of heaven. (Matthew 5:3)

Goals for Growth

- Reject self-sufficiency as a core value in my life.
- Develop an attitude of deep dependence upon God.
- Practice surrendering to God out of love for Him and experience His blessings as a result.

Head Start

As a kid I (Kenny) could get on my dad's good side by doing certain things. Mowing the lawn. Cleaning the garage. Taking the trash to the curb before he pulled in from work. I was on a point system, and I knew what brought a double bonus of Dad's favor. I could earn my way into a couple of bucks, or permission to stay out late, as long as there was enough "Kenny credit" in Dad's recent memory bank. It was really that simple.

The point system transferred to many other areas of my life as well, and I could pretty much count on being promptly and generously rewarded for my performance. In school I figured out how to work the system for good grades. In sports I practiced and trained hard—and got rewarded. I had three jobs in high school, so I'd always have enough money. Socially, it was no different. Say the right things, show up at the right places, participate in the right activities (or in my case, the wrong activities), and I'd end up winning friends and influencing people. All I had to do was bring myself to the table, take the right actions, and I was "in." I always had a stake in my own success. College—the same. Career—the same. Marriage— the same.

At some level, don't all men like to think we control our own destinies? It's in our DNA. We make our own blessings—or so we think.

And our culture constantly encourages this attitude because it has branded self-sufficiency as a positive attribute. Is it any surprise, then, that Americans take fewer vacations than citizens of any other country? We chafe at extended periods away from work. We get the shakes.

The world may take this view, but God does not. God's blessings, joy, and kingdom are not received, Jesus says, by conquest. They are bestowed when we surrender. Just like a hungry beggar who has nowhere else to turn and goes to the rescue mission looking for help, so we come to God with palms upturned, ready to receive, because our need has overcome our pride.

We have no illusions; we are poor.

We have no pride, only need.

We recognize that we have nothing to offer and are open to receiving help.

Men who live large spiritually are those who know they're in trouble. That's the attitude of God's man. That's what it means to be "poor in spirit" (Matthew 5:3).

Connect with the Word

Read Matthew 5:3.

1. Why does a man need to become poor in spirit in order to experience a solid connection with God and His purposes? What is the opposite of poor in spirit? TO PUT YOUR VALUES ON THE THINGS OF THIS EARTH AND NOT ON THE HEAVENLY THINGS.
B) MATERIALISM, PRIDE ~ SELF CENTERDNESS

2. Why do you think Jesus started the Beatitudes with this trait? BECAUSE HE PROBABLY WAS THE ONE ARE WE STRUGGLE MOST WITH. WE CANNOT WORK OUR WAY TO HEAVEN; THINGS WE DO ~ WE MUST HAVE DEPENDENCE ON HIM TO BE RICH. IT IS A GIFT - MOST OF US HAVE IT WRONG.

3. Name some of the people Jesus met and blessed who were poor in spirit. What characterized His interactions with them? What

do you learn from them? (As an example, see Matthew 8:1-13 and 9:18-30.) *THE TAX COLLECTOR, THE WOMAN AT THE WELL, THE BLIND MAN AT THE TEMPLE*

4. When have you felt the most poor in spirit? How did this affect your attitudes, circumstances, and spiritual growth?

   DURING MY FIRST MARRIAGE — IT WAS RUINED

Read James 4:6-10.

5. According to verse 6, what kind of person does God connect with the best?

   THOSE WHO ARE HUMBLE, NOT PROUD

6. What actions do we need to take to humble ourselves before the Lord so that He will lift us up (verses 7-9)? Give an example or two of how this has played out in your own life over the years.

   PURIFY OUR HEARTS AND WASH OUR HAND. (METAPHORICLLY) - REMOVE THINGS FROM OUR LIVES THAT ARE IMPURE.
   A) DON'T WATCH BAD MOVIES
   DON'T ~~USE~~ GOSSIP.
   LOVE YOUR ENEMIES

7. In what practical ways does a man need to resist the devil?

   STAY AWAY FROM THINGS THAT ARE IMPURE. CHANGE OUR THOUGHTS AND ACTIONS

8. According to verse 8, what perspective should we have about ourselves?

   THAT WE ARE SINNERS, SEPARATED FROM GOD. WE ARE WICKED

9. What actions are required of God's man to make change possible for him (verse 8)? What needs to change? Why?

   WE NEED TO COME NEAR TO GOD AND PURGE OURSELVES FROM THINGS THAT ARE EVIL.

10. According to verse 9, what kinds of emotions flow when a man realizes the depth of his sin of self-sufficiency?

    SHAME AND GRIEF

11. Describe a defining moment of self-humbling in your life—or a defining event of self-sufficiency. How did things unfold? What did you learn about life? yourself? God?

Connect with the Group

Group Opener
Read the group opener aloud and discuss the questions that follow. (Suggestion: As you begin your group discussion time in each of the following sessions, consider forming smaller groups of three to six men. This will allow more time for discussion and give everyone an opportunity to share their thoughts and struggles.)

The intensive care unit at Mercy Hospital is not the place you want to be on New Year's Eve, but that is where my brother, Chris, and I [Kenny] found ourselves on that holiday evening one year. We were at the hospital because our dad had been admitted, and in the morning, he would be rolled into a surgical bay to undergo quadruple bypass surgery. For Chris and me, it was nervous time, as Los Angeles Lakers radio announcer Chick Hearn used to say, because we weren't sure if Dad would make it. Chris and I had been told that our disoriented father could wake up and try to pull out some of the IV lines regulating his heart rate and blood pressure, so we were on guard for that eventuality.

We were surprised when one of Dad's longtime friends, a great guy named Greg, joined us for the all-night vigil. As we sat together in the ICU, my brother and I listened as Greg talked about growing up in a church where God was portrayed as The Rule Guy, a cosmic policeman who loves nothing better than punishing slackers unable to keep up with His program. Combined with his own father's propensities toward anger and abuse, Greg's image of Father God was, shall we say, a little distorted. Naturally, there was no room in his life for matters of faith. Greg had decided long ago that the Father, Son, and Holy Spirit were meaningless apparitions for him.

The turning point in our conversation came when we discussed the actions of the son and the father in the story of the prodigal son. I remember saying that the son returned home covered in pig slop, which was an apt metaphor for all the messes we make in life. Nothing like a little barnyard stench to get you feeling humble. But once humbled, the son presented himself to his father, admitted his mistake, and asked for a job as a slave with no privileges. Instead of blasting his son for blowing all his inheritance on wine, women, and song, the father ran to him, melted into his arms, and called for a celebration. "This son of mine was dead and has now returned to life," he proclaimed (Luke 15:24, NLT).

Everything changed for the son because he was willing to humble himself before the truth of his circumstances and before his father, who was waiting eagerly for him to return.

The language Jesus used in the parable shocked people then, just as it rocked Greg's image of God at 3 A.M. in the ICU. It had never dawned on Greg that God loved and cared for him—one of His sons—and was waiting for him to come back into His arms.

When men get it—really get it—that God, who is superior in all ways, also cares deeply for them, humility finds a home in their hearts.[1]

---

1. Stephen Arterburn and Kenny Luck, *Every Man, God's Man* (Colorado Springs: WaterBrook, 2003), 124-25.

Discussion Questions

a. How do you think Greg got the impression from church that God is "The Rule Guy"? Have you ever felt that way? Explain.

FROM HIS OWN FATHER'S ACTIONS AND WHAT HE HEARD IN CHURCH, HE FELT THAT WHAT WAS THE DEFENITION OF "FATHER".

b. What key truth can a man discover about God that will give him a humble heart?

THAT GOD BECAME MAN TO DIE FOR US, HE LOVED US THAT MUCH AND NO MATTER HOW MUCH WE FAIL, HE STILL LOVES US.

c. In what ways do you battle self-sufficiency? What can you do to develop more of an attitude of dependence on God?

WE WORRY TOO MUCH ABOUT WHAT WE CAN'T CHANGE AND TRY TO SOLVE THINGS ON OUR OWN AND NOT TRUST GOD.

d. To what extent has humility found a home in your heart? If possible, share a specific example.

WHEN I LOST MY JOB ~ PRIDE WAS MY SIN. ACHIEVING SUCCESS! NOT HAVING HUMILITY.

e. How does God use the problems and trials we face in our lives to bring us to a place of humility? Share an example of this in your own experience. SAME AS PREVIOUS ANSWER

f. In the most practical terms, how can we apply James's command to humble ourselves before the Lord?

g. How will the practice of humbling ourselves daily before the Lord result in our being lifted up? (See James 4:10.)

h. What have you found to be the most effective way to resist the devil when he tempts you with pride? What advice in this area could you give the other guys?

i. What do you think you need to surrender to God in order to experience His promised blessings?

Standing Strong

As you look back over your life so far, ask yourself, What have I needed that only God can give? Make a list. Then thank the Lord for providing those specific things that your own efforts could not supply.

Based upon what you have learned in this session about being poor in spirit, write a brief prayer to God in the space below. Then humble yourself and share your prayer with others in the group.

100 percent wrong!

God's Man Repents from the Heart

Key Verse

Blessed are those who mourn, for they will be comforted.
(Matthew 5:4)

Goals for Growth

- Call on God to do what I can't do myself.
- Express sorrow over choosing my own path and plans.
- Demonstrate true repentance in my attitudes and actions.

Head Start

The world says happiness should be your goal, and nothing should keep you from it. God says brokenness comes before blessing. The world says you should avoid pain at all costs. God says some pain is necessary for growth and character development. The world teaches, "Never let them see you cry." Jesus says, "Mourn." The world says, "Love means never having to say you're sorry." God says, "You can't experience true love and intimacy with Me until you say you're sorry for trying to *be* Me."

It's one thing to *say* you're sorry, but it's another thing to *feel* sorrow. Words are easy. Take my (Kenny's) son, Ryan, for example. Caught red-handed picking on his little sister, he hears my command to apologize. I immediately hear "Sorry, Jenna" offered in the most nonchalant tone. For him, the words are a get-out-of-jail-free card; the insincerity fries me.

So I sometimes make him rewind the tape and do it again until I feel his apology to little Jenna is more genuine. After all, no one who deserves a sincere apology appreciates hollow words.

Most of the men I counsel week to week have a big problem admitting failure. The world's emphasis on happiness at all costs—and on keeping up one's image—makes men say things they don't mean, deny problems that are glaringly obvious, and seek escape from difficult situations instead of trying to resolve them. These men simply don't want to risk the discomfort. They don't like their lack of control over people's responses. They don't want to experience the real consequences of their unsavory actions. Most of all, they don't want to grieve over their failure to please God, nor do they want to do what the Bible calls them to do: repent.

Yet our failure *does* call for mourning...and changing. Right after Jesus dropped the first torpedo in the water ("Don't act as if you've got it together"), He launched another beauty: "You're 100 percent wrong!"

Wrong about what? you ask.

Answer: We're wrong for thinking we can run the life He gave us independent of His plan, that we can actually prosper with such an approach. When we've offended God the Father, just saying "sorry" doesn't cut it. But sorrow-motivated *change* does. That's what true repentance involves. And like my son, Ryan, all God's boys will have to rewind the tape many, many times on the way to growing up in Him. Men who live large spiritually are those who repent sincerely—and as often as needed.

Connect with the Word

Read Matthew 5:4.

1. Why do you think Jesus spoke about mourning immediately after his discussion of being poor in spirit?

2. How does blessedness (joy) flow from deep sadness?

3. What obstacles seem to prevent men from feeling the depth of the wrong they've done against God and people?

4. Where do you find comfort when you are mourning? How does this help—or hurt?

Read Psalm 51.

5. What did David need from God? Describe a time in your life when you could most relate to David's need.

6. According to verse 6, what did David know that God wanted from him?

7. What did David ask God to do in response to David's sincere admission of sin (verses 10-11)?

8. What did David know would eventually come from his sadness and sorrow before God (verse 12)?

9. What is the main ingredient of godly sorrow (verse 17)? Why is this essential?

Connect with the Group

Group Opener
Discuss the group-opener questions and the discussion questions that follow.

In what area(s) of your life recently have you had to admit failure, express sorrow, or ask for God's forgiveness and help?

What role has godly sorrow played in your spiritual growth over the years?

Discussion Questions

a. Why are we reluctant to mourn (express sorrow over our wrongs) in front of other people? Why should we not be reluctant to mourn before God?

b. How do you think God knows we have meant it from our hearts when we say we're sorry over wrong choices?

c. What happens when we turn to God with our sorrow and sin? How, specifically, does He comfort us?

d. How can you tell when you have a broken and contrite heart? Do you find it hard or easy to let God comfort you? Explain.

e. What's the difference between helping a broken man and a prideful man? What does the future hold for each?

Standing Strong

Read slowly through Psalm 51:1-17 and make it your personal prayer. Pause at verse 3 and think through the areas in your life that are out of alignment (or ask God to reveal those areas to you in the days ahead). Finally, ask a trusted friend to identify any areas in your life where he sees a need for repentance so that you can address them.

As you think about the areas you and your friend identified, ask God to give you a spirit of brokenness and godly sorrow about them. Write down some practical steps you will take to deal with these areas in your life.

Share with your group any areas needing repentance that God has revealed to you. As you are led, invite the guys in your group to hold you accountable or counsel you as you take concrete steps to repent in those areas.

hand over the keys

God's Man Relinquishes Control Willingly

Key Verse

Blessed are the meek, for they will inherit the earth. (Matthew 5:5)

Goals for Growth

- Reject the myth that meek is weak.
- Place my life in God's hands for shaping.
- Become a conduit of God's power to accomplish His purposes.

Head Start

Jesus said, "I am gentle and humble in heart" (Matthew 11:29). The world says that meek is weak. After all, look at what happened to Jesus!

For many people in Jesus's day, piety was all about power. Is it any different today? Think about it: Power is all about control. The more power you wield, the more control you can exert over people and circumstances. The more control you possess, the more you can manipulate people and circumstances in your favor. The more you manipulate the world around you, the more predictable your life becomes. The more predictable your life becomes (or so the myth goes), the fewer surprises you'll encounter. And when you know what's coming, circumstances and emotions never spiral out of control. Control is the crack cocaine of the power game.

When God's man recognizes he's not God (becomes poor in spirit) and repents of (mourns) his self-sufficiency, what does Jesus say to him? "Blessed are the meek."

The next step is about giving up total control over our lives. "Hand over the keys," Jesus says. "I'm taking the wheel, so slide over." As God's man slides over and lets God take control of his life, he becomes meek. He becomes a man who God can shape, mold, guide, and lead. The meek man is a tool, or instrument, in God's hands as he willingly allows the Master Craftsman to work powerfully in and through him.

It's like when a former customer asked the local ex-barber, "Why did you change professions and become a painter?" The ex-barber replied, "Because the canvas doesn't tell me how to make it beautiful!" A meek man is the canvas. He is not a pushover or a doormat, however. God is not against a man's having power and influence. But God knows the pain that unrestrained power can cause a flawed human being, and He wants to help us manage it for His purposes.

The best example of this kind of power-under-God's-control is illustrated in the life of Jesus Christ. He showed us all the power of meekness when He prayed, "Not my will, but yours be done" (Luke 22:42) as He faced the cross. He courageously embraced suffering of infinite proportions so that He might pay for our sins.

Could you have left the comforts and glories of heaven to immerse yourself in the grunge and grime of the human heart?

Do you still think meek is weak?

Connect with the Word

Read Matthew 5:5.

1. Imagine being God for a moment. Why do You put a premium on meekness?

2. How does being biblically meek bless God's man?

3. What do you think it means to "inherit the earth"? What problems do you think the original listeners would have had with this characterization of meekness? What are our own hang-ups with it?

4. Think about the kind of men Jesus surrounded Himself with. Do you think they were meek? Why or why not?

5. In light of God's desire to develop meekness in you, what conclusions does it lead you to make about God's priorities?

Read James 5:17.

6. What does this verse say about Elijah?

7. What determined how powerfully God used Elijah: his ability or his availability? Explain.

8. What does being available to God mean to you in practical terms? Available for what?

9. When in the past have you made yourself available to God? What happened as a result?

10. How does our availability to be used by God demonstrate meekness before Him?

Connect with the Group

Group Opener

Read the group opener aloud and discuss the questions that follow.

Three years ago at a men's retreat, I [Kenny] saw a man decide to eliminate the wavering in his walk with Jesus. Phil told me he knew what needed to be done to become God's man. First, he verbally articulated the path he wanted to take. Next, he made himself accountable to several men and me. From that day forward, he began acting in faith.

Phil did that by joining a men's Bible study that met before work one morning each week. He began to tithe faithfully. He began to consciously invest more time and energy in his marriage and family. He began to risk letting his faith come out in everyday conversations and standing firmly in Christ's camp. He started praying dangerously by asking God to use him in ministry. After agreeing to lead a couples Bible study in his home on Thursday nights, he approached me about getting involved with Every Man Ministries, which led to his becoming a board member. Phil was trusting fully—no stash of self-reliance in his closet.

I beamed with pride the day Phil stood before two hundred men and declared, "As men we love to risk. We love a good challenge—a mountain to climb, a distance to be traveled. We love the win. We like how winning makes us feel and how it makes us look to others. Well, that was me—I loved the win as well. I would risk everything for the sale, but tragically, I would risk nothing for my Savior. But now, with God's help and the support of you, I am risking more for Jesus."

Is Phil's faith perfect?

No.

Is he identifying areas of change, getting God's directions and plan, and pursuing those changes before God and man?

Yes. He is responding to God in faith.

And that's a great place to be.[2]

---

2.   Arterburn and Luck, *Every Man, God's Man,* 70-71.

Discussion Questions

a. Think through the steps Phil took in order to straighten out his walk with Jesus. Which step(s) would have been most difficult for you to take? Why?

b. How do you see meekness demonstrated in Phil's decisions?

c. When God's man knows he's in God's hands, what effect should that have on his confidence level? Explain.

d. In what area of your life is it hardest for you to give up control? Why is it so tough to place that issue under God's control and influence?

e. What victories or pains encourage you to yield more and more areas of your life to God's control?

f. What problems has God used in your life to make you more moldable?

Standing Strong
List areas of your life over which you have resisted giving God complete control.

Pray the following prayer over the areas you listed and fully release them to God:

"God, not my will but Your will be done with _____ (area listed). Show me what You want me to do, and help me obey."

Repeat this prayer often, then write down your action steps as God reveals them.

Action God Requires   *Action Step I Will Take This Week*

cravings satisfied in God

God's Man Redefines Contentment

Key Verse

Blessed are those who hunger and thirst for righteousness, for they will be filled. (Matthew 5:6)

Goals for Growth

- Develop a deep personal hunger for God's purposes.
- Diminish appetites for things that do not satisfy.
- Experience contentment in being God's man.

Head Start

Contentment. Fulfillment. Peace. Purpose. Significance. Satisfaction. Jesus knew that every man strives to get his fill of these elusive delights. So He said, "Blessed are those who hunger and thirst for righteousness, for they will be filled." But even though this statement is crystal clear, millions of men who call themselves Christians are hedging their bets on Christ's proposition. They're holding out. They're exploring alternative paths to contentment. And in the process, they—and everyone around them—suffer.

How do I (Kenny) know? Sadly, I've learned from personal experience. For a span of time, I was one of those suckers the world ripped off. I swallowed all the lies and drove my life into the ditch in the process. My poor wife watched me offer myself upon the altar of materialism and plunge us into financial bondage. She watched me project a public image that said, "Everything's fine," while my home life was disintegrating. She watched me drink at what author Max Lucado calls the "false fountains" of "just a little more" and "if only."

The entire time, God lovingly ignored my pleas for more financial bonuses and wisely kept me from being promoted. He knew I didn't have the character to manage those blessings—yet. He knew my heart would become too strongly attached to them and that I'd forget Him in the mix. He knew the real solution: I needed to look to Him and be obedient to His direction. Only then would He fill the empty place in me that I longed for the world to meet.

Jesus knows that after a man recognizes his need (becomes poor in spirit), repents sincerely (mourns and takes steps to change), and surrenders total control to God (becomes meek), he needs a new path to travel. He needs a calling he can pour his heart into, some cause that will bring lasting rather than temporary fulfillment. He needs a purpose that is significant. So Jesus tells him exactly how to get lasting satisfaction: Jump onto the path of righteousness. And pursue it with the passion and hunger of a starving bear.

In other words, let God's purposes consume you. The result? Contentment. Fulfillment. Peace. Purpose. Significance. Satisfaction.

Connect with the Word

Read Matthew 5:6.

1. Why do you think Jesus used "hunger and thirst" to describe the important quality of righteousness in His followers?

2. What did Jesus know about people that makes this statement especially meaningful? What two types of hunger was He comparing?

3. What does hungering and thirsting for righteousness mean to you personally? Write this beatitude in your own words.

4. What happens when we choose to drink at "false fountains"? List some of those drinking places that tempt you the most.

Read John 4:1-18.

5. What did Jesus know about the woman at the well? What kind of water did she really need?

6. According to verse 10, how did Jesus get to the heart of the matter: the woman's quest for fulfillment and purpose?

7. What did Jesus mean when he said, "Everyone who drinks this water will be thirsty again, but whoever drinks the water I give him will never thirst" (verses 13-14)? What thirst can He alone satisfy?

8. After a person drinks of the water Jesus gives, what begins to happen in that person's life (verse 14)?

9. In what ways is the image of "a spring of water welling up" helpful and powerful for you?

Connect with the Group

Group Opener

Discuss the group-opener question and the discussion questions that follow.

What have you discovered to be a false fountain in your life? Talk about what happens when you turn to this polluted watering hole for spiritual fulfillment.

Discussion Questions

a. What circumstances does God seem to use to get you to stop looking for purpose and fulfillment apart from Him?

b. Why do you think so many men keep going back to false fountains for more when they know these fountains don't satisfy?

c. What role does God's Word play in helping you seek the true Source of fulfillment?

d. What keeps you from filling up on God? What temptations or diversions call out the loudest to you? In what situations?

e. Since Jesus knows what satisfies God's man and what doesn't, in what direction will He always lead you? In what real-life situations have you found this to be true?

f. Do men have to stop dreaming and/or desiring in order to fulfill God's purposes? Talk about it.

g. What does being filled or satisfied in God look like to you in daily life? Give one or two specific examples.

Standing Strong

List the false fountains you are tempted to drink from to find fulfillment.

List the people, places, and activities that help you hunger and thirst for righteousness—and find it.

Ask God right now to give you a stronger heart for His purposes. Ask Him to show you the dangers of false fountains.

mercy unplugged

God's Man Releases Others Regularly

Key Verse

Blessed are the merciful, for they will be shown mercy. (Matthew 5:7)

Goals for Growth

- Remember my own sinful condition and my need for God's mercy.
- Reflect on God's mercy shown us in Christ.
- Renew my commitment to be an instrument of mercy to others.

Head Start

The world says, "They deserve to be punished." God says, "So do you." We've seen that Jesus started the Beatitudes with matters of the heart. Changes in the heart (becoming poor in spirit, mourning our sins, and becoming meek) lead to a change of purpose (having a hunger and thirst for God's righteous will). Next, the acid test of our faith is how we work His will into all our relationships. Will we reproduce our experience with God in the relationships He's given us? In the fifth beatitude, Jesus goes for the jugular vein of relationships: the issue of mercy or forgiveness.

Men seem to love being in the "six position." That's fighter-pilot-speak for flying directly behind the other guy, locked on, with guns selected. Some men just can't resist that little red trigger switch, and they regularly allow their brains to signal their thumbs. They squeeze down, ignoring the inner voice of reason and the call of the Holy Spirit. Somehow they've failed to see the new weapon in their arsenal—a spiritual weapon that does far more good than the other options. It's called forgiveness.

Recently I (Kenny) asked more than two hundred guys to reflect on their salvation experience and share it with one another. When I asked, "What was your most memorable feeling?" the vast majority said it was the feeling of being forgiven and the freedom it brought to their hearts. Yet when I asked whether they were stingy or liberal with extending forgiveness and mercy to others, you could have heard a pin drop. Why? Perhaps it's because we forget how God so extravagantly lavished His mercy on us even though we didn't deserve it. He held back dishing out the punishment our sins did deserve. Instead, to our eternal and grateful relief, He came to the table with kindness, compassion, and mercy.

Do we have salvation amnesia? How else could we tolerate our own blatant refusal to follow Christ by being willing channels of forgiveness?

Jesus knew that imperfect, flawed people need lots of mercy. He also knew that the mercy factor requires teeth and accountability. He didn't mince words about it, saying, in effect, "I love it when you splash gobs of mercy on everyone around you." And why shouldn't we do that? After all, we will receive mercy in the same measure that we spread it around.

So when it comes to mercy, are you liberal or stingy?

Connect with the Word

Read Matthew 5:7.

1. Why is the quality of mercy so important to God?

2. What should motivate us to be willing agents of God's mercy?

3. In what ways are we blessed when we choose to forgive and release others?

4. What was Jesus implying when He said, "for [the merciful] will be shown mercy"?

5. What positive impact for God can mercy have upon the recipient? When have you experienced this or seen it happen to someone else?

Read Titus 3:1-8.

6. When is "show[ing] true humility toward all men" (verse 2) most difficult for you?

7. What purpose do you think Titus's mentor had in mind when he wrote verse 3? What was Paul attempting to do? Whom did Paul include in the group he was describing?

8. Was God liberal or stingy with His mercy (verse 6)? Explain.

9. What did God's mercy and grace ultimately provide for us (verse 7)?

10. According to verse 8, what should be the result of remembering how mercifully God saved us?

Connect with the Group

Group Opener
Read the group opener aloud and discuss the questions that follow.

Without much help from his family, Danny paid his way through college and landed a sales job with a copier company. His self-discipline and natural sales skills rocketed him to the position of top producer in the western region. Five promotions and seven years later, his office overlooked San Francisco Bay and Alcatraz Island. He had married his college sweetheart, Beth Anne, and they had a beautiful baby girl with another on the way. They lived among some of the most influential venture-capital and high-tech people in America. By all accounts, however, Danny was earning something more than his high-six-figure salary: a reputation for being ruthless. Behind his back, employees called him "Darth Vader." Either his guys hit their numbers or they hit the road—no exceptions.

One Sunday morning, Curt, a junior sales executive at Danny's company, was surprised to see Danny at church. The two had just met at the annual sales conference. Curt spotted him at the coffee bar outside the foyer and made a beeline over to him.

"You go to church here?" he said, not knowing how Danny would respond.

"I've been coming here since we moved from Texas ten years ago," Danny replied.

"I didn't know you were a Christian," Curt blurted out, somewhat excited about the prospect that the top sales exec in his company was a believer.

Danny ignored the remark. "You work for Cameron, don't you?" he said, referring to one of the sales managers.

"Yes, I do. In fact, you should pray for him," Curt urged.

"Why? What's going on?"

"Well, you probably already know this," Curt answered, visibly subdued, "but his wife's cancer is back, and he's devastated."

"I had no idea," Danny said. He had seen Cameron just a few days earlier when he chewed him out for arriving late for the quarterly sales meeting. Cameron had mentioned something about his wife being ill, but Danny's focus had been on the fourth-quarter drop in Cameron's production. Silently, he reprimanded himself for being so unfeeling and unneighborly.[3]

Discussion Questions

a. Like Danny, when have you been given an opportunity to extend compassion and mercy but failed? Tell the group about it.

b. What keeps us from extending mercy to others when they need it?

c. How do the dark parts of our lives give us a deeper realization of God's mercy toward us? (Be as specific as you can.)

---

3. Arterburn and Luck, *Every Man, God's Man*, 64-65.

d. What does it feel like to experience mercy? When have you been the most overwhelmed by the mercy God or others have extended to you?

e. Is the experience of God's mercy a one-time event or an ongoing process? Explain.

f. What is the best way to thank God for His mercy? Give a specific example of how you do this.

Standing Strong

In a few moments of silence, meditate on these two statements: Mercy is deserved punishment held back. Grace is undeserved favor poured out.

Pray and thank God for saving you by His mercy and grace.

Make a list of all the good things God has brought into your life through His mercy and grace.

To whom can you extend mercy today? (Jot some names below and make yourself accountable to the group by sharing your plans.)

the great pretender or the real deal?

God's Man Rejects Self-Deception

Key Verse

Blessed are the pure in heart, for they will see God. (Matthew 5:8)

Goals for Growth

- Assess my level of honesty with myself, God, and others.
- Deal directly with issues of the heart that cause dishonesty.
- Pursue authenticity in all my relationships.

Head Start

We love clinging to first impressions. We love profiling people based on what they wear, what they drive, and what they do for a living.

In fact, most of us are willing to swallow appearances without question, and I (Kenny) confess that I'm as guilty as the next guy. Men are notoriously poor judges of people. We're visual and performance-oriented. So if a guy looks okay on the surface and produces good results (or even looks as if he could), then we tend to give him high marks.

The world thrives on image over substance, on our efforts to get others to think we're someone we're not. For us guys, our public self is tied to what we do, and we feel safest when talking about professional stuff. Or we'll let the conversation drift over to sports and hobbies since these topics are also "safe."

Sadly, our public image is easy to maintain because those watching aren't closely connected to us. It doesn't take much character to maintain a shallow persona. The public guy we present never talks about any of his real problems or failings. Why? Because the image would implode upon itself, revealing the real man inside.

Commenting on our propensity to create public images and hide the real man, Brennan Manning writes in his book *Reflections for Ragamuffins*, "Those of us who play this game wear a thousand masks to disguise the face of fear." To that powerful observation I would add, "But every man's mask is transparent." You see, men who play this game aren't fooling anyone close to them, especially their Creator. Nevertheless, the world continues encouraging our masquerade.

In stark contrast to the world's message, Jesus throws down the gauntlet in our relationship with Him and calls to us, "Take off the mask. If you are to live large spiritually, then you don't need to cover up. Because I know you—the real you."

The challenge for us is to quit pretending, to end all the silly imposter games we play. For Jesus says, "I can't connect with people who are self-deceived—lying to themselves and others and attempting to play Me, too!"

The honest, not the self-deceived, connect with Jesus Christ. They get to "see" Him clearly, hear Him in the stillness, and relate to Him closely. The key that unlocks this kind of intimacy with God is brutal honesty coupled with a willingness to open all that we are to Him. It's called purity of heart.

Connect with the Word

Read Matthew 5:8.

1. The heart represents our motives and desires. Why does the condition of our hearts matter so much to God?

2. What does *pure* mean to you? Why is it a prerequisite to connecting with God?

3. What do you think seeing God means in practical terms?

4. Why do men struggle with being completely open and honest with one another, even as brothers in Christ? When do you see this happening most often?

Read Psalm 139:23-24.

5. Would you call David's prayer a courageous one? Why or why not?

6. What was David asking God to test? Why?

7. What did David want in his relationship with God? To what extent do you want this too? How can you tell?

8. On a scale of 1 to 10 (1 = totally closed; 10 = completely open), what do you think was David's level of openness to feedback? Explain.

9. What does David's prayer tell us about his relationship with God? How does it relate to Matthew 5:8?

10. What would it take for you to pray this kind of prayer, holding nothing back from the Lord?

Connect with the Group

Group Opener
Discuss the group-opener question and the discussion questions that follow.

Which of the following is your biggest heart struggle? Why?

____ honesty with self

____ honesty with others

____ honesty with God

Discussion Questions

a. Jesus directs us to deal with the tough issues of the heart. What do the world and the devil try to get us to focus on?

b. Why do you think most men feel that if they can change their circumstances (i.e., get a new relationship, job, toy, bank account, etc.), they will change inwardly, too?

c. Why don't external fixes actually fix us?

d. How does getting honest with ourselves, God, and others make a difference in our lives? What does it do for us? What does it do for those we love or those who love us?

e. When we "clean house" spiritually, what, in addition to God, do we see more clearly?

f. When, if ever, have you prayed a prayer like the one David prayed in Psalm 139? Which area(s) of your life is most difficult for you to open up to God?

g. What area of your life, if any, has God shown you about which you are in denial or are not being honest with yourself? What do you think He wants you to do?

Standing Strong

In which area(s) of your life would you like to be more honest with yourself, God, and others? Write it down below and share it with your group.

In the following space, write the name of one person in your group whom you will give special permission to ask questions and give you advice concerning this area. Sign and date this agreement, and commit to listen closely to his advice. (*Note:* Before you ask this man to help with your accountability, read James 5:16 and Psalm 101.)

"I give _____ permission to ask me any questions and offer godly advice about my struggle."

Signed:_____ Date: _____

comparing, competing, or connecting?

God's Man Reconciles Relationships

Key Verse

Blessed are the peacemakers, for they will be called sons of God. (Matthew 5:9)

Goals for Growth

- Eliminate bitterness and resentment as controlling influences in my life.
- Stop comparing, competing, and being critical.
- See others through God's eyes in order to connect with them.

Head Start

It all starts on the playground when we're little boys. For some reason it's critically important to be first in line for everything. We're always jockeying for position, always trying to one-up our buddies—"My dad's so strong, he could whip yours with one hand tied behind his back." Or maybe we're always trying to get a bigger laugh than the other guy.

What is it that pushes us to compete so furiously with one another? It's not a bad mind-set to take to the gridiron or a track meet, but it generates conflict and resentment in our everyday relationships. Worse, when we're comparing and measuring ourselves against the other guy, there's little chance we'll ever connect with him on a meaningful level. So we keep each other at a distance, even in the church. Every man is his own nation, it seems, complete with borders and protective fences. We've adopted a mentality that says, "I must not get close to you or let you get close to me."

And what about our relationships with women? Your lovely princess may tolerate competitive behavior (such as dominating her at miniature golf) when you're dating, but cutting down your wife in front of her friends—because that's what you do with the guys—invites a whole new form of disaster. Our bent for comparing and competing is so ingrained that many of us can't tone it down in our relationship with the woman God has called us to encourage and serve.

The sad result? Millions of marriages are floundering.

Men just don't do this connection thing very well—that is, the meaningful, nonphysical type of connection that cultivates intimacy and friendship with both sexes. And it's killing us!

But gentlemen, Jesus's words give us tremendous hope. We may not be natural-born peacemakers, but we can learn to connect with others by developing our connection with God. More important, we have Christ, who is our capable teacher and model, and our personal experience of reconciliation with Him to help us. It's as if Jesus is asking us, "Want to know the surest sign of your closeness to Me?" If we say yes, He'll tell us: "It's the power I've given you to overcome conflict and achieve deep connection with others."

A child of God is a peacemaker, but not because he's good at it. He fights to connect with others because Jesus died to connect him with the Father.

Connect with the Word

Read Matthew 5:9.

1. In your experience, what opportunities do conflicts in relationships provide?

2. What does peacemaking look like in your own life on a daily basis?

3. In what ways are we blessed when we make every effort to reestablish connection with others?

4. Why did Jesus describe peacemaking as a quality that identifies us directly with God?

5. Jesus often connected with people who were labeled as outcasts as well as those who felt unworthy of His attention. How did He do it? What can you learn from Him in this regard?

6. Why do you think Jesus assigned the title "sons of God" to peacemakers? Why might that title appeal to men?

Read James 3:13-18.

7. What two lifestyles was James contrasting here?

8. What attitude must we have in order to live out a lifestyle of reconciliation (verse 13)?

9. What are the outcomes of the me-first lifestyle (verse 16)?

10. What qualities characterize and complement the peacemaker (verse 17)?

11. What multiplying effect of peacemaking is described in verse 18?

12. Do you hear a call to action in this passage? If so, what is it saying to you?

Connect with the Group

Group Opener
Read the group opener aloud and discuss the questions that follow.

Patrick used...misguided logic when he started complaining to his wife, Elise, about their relationship. Sure, their marriage had seen better days, but the stress of Patrick's working nights and Elise's working days was threatening to blow the top off the relationship. Earlier in the marriage, Patrick had supported Elise through medical school, putting off his law enforcement career plans. He had never complained, willingly devoting himself to the kids who came along and to Elise's medical career. He had even led his wife to Christ. But lately his faith had been strangely absent.

Once Elise had finished up her internship, Patrick resumed his quest to join the California Highway Patrol. After filing all the paperwork, undergoing a battery of background interviews, and passing a series of tests, Patrick was welcomed to the force. As a rookie, however, Patrick was slotted into the graveyard shift, patrolling Southern California's perpetually busy freeways from 11 P.M. to 7 A.M.

Patrick and Elise were like ships passing in the night, able to see each other only for the handful of hours between dinnertime and his night shift. Patrick became moodier, and whenever Elise would try to get close, he would push her away. Innocent inquiries into the job were labeled inquisitions, and Elise remained in the dark. Patrick's only family involvement was showing up for the kids' soccer games.

Elise felt her husband was purposely creating distance. With each passing day, a dark shadow lengthened over the relationship. She tried to ignore her doubts until the day she came home for lunch on one of Patrick's off days to discover that her intuition was correct: He was in bed with another woman.

"How could you?" Elise railed after the woman dressed and left.

"I haven't loved you for the last two years," Patrick snipped. He meant it to hurt.

"What's going on with you? Some midlife crisis?" she countered.

"All these years it's been about you, and you never once offered to support me with the CHP. That's why I did it on my own. I knew you wouldn't approve."

"You never gave me a chance. You kept me in the dark."

"Listen," Patrick said. "I don't care, and I don't care about you."

Pausing and shaking her head, Elise looked Patrick straight in the eye. "Is that the best you can do? Is that what you are going to tell the kids? Is that what you are going to tell God?"

What is Patrick going to say to the Lord who knows all our thoughts?[4]

Discussion Questions

a. Imagine for a moment that you are Patrick. How did you allow the dark shadow of distance and separation to enter your marital relationship? What do you think you'll do about it?

---

4. Arterburn and Luck, *Every Man, God's Man,* 50-52.

b. What one quality is most important to maintaining connection in the midst of conflict?

c. What do we learn from Christ's efforts on our behalf about what is necessary for making peace? What did He have to do to secure our peace with God?

d. What are some practical ways you've been able to "sow" peace in your relationships over the years? What actions, habits, and words seem to work best?

e. What role does the condition of your heart play when you're trying to make peace with others? Give a practical example, if possible.

f. When you're in conflict with someone, how hard or easy is it for you to look in the mirror first? Explain. How does ownership of your part in the conflict facilitate peacemaking?

g. What role does prayer play in peacemaking? How can it change your approach, actions, or reactions during conflict situations?

Standing Strong

List the relationships in your life in which you would like to see deeper connection instead of separation. Pray for the people you listed.

Read and memorize James 1:19. Ask God to give you the power to follow His instructions in this verse.

risking pain for the highest purpose

God's Man Risks Disapproval from Other Men

Key Verses

Blessed are those who are persecuted because of righteousness, for theirs is the kingdom of heaven. Blessed are you when people insult you, persecute you and falsely say all kinds of evil against you because of me. (Matthew 5:10-11)

Goals for Growth

- Fear men—and the opinions of men—less.
- Consistently make choices that demonstrate loyalty to Christ.
- Suffer willingly for Christ when I face persecution in His name.

Head Start

The world says, "You are a religious fanatic." God says, "You are a loyal son." The world says, "People think you're weird." God says, "I think you're incredible." The world says, "You're no fun." God says, "I approve of the way you're living." The world says, "You're intolerant and narrow-minded." Jesus says, "I am the Way, and you will be blessed because you follow Me."

The majority of us live our lives trying to avoid emotional and physical suffering, right? We buy cars with air bags. We get flu shots to prevent disease. We avoid interpersonal confrontations. The psychology of our culture is one of prevention, protection, safety, tolerance, peace, diversity, and we keep developing new ways to advance in these areas. Is it any wonder, then, that when it comes to willingly signing up to suffer, most of us hesitate? It's not an acceptable career hazard. Personal preservation is the name of the game.

Jesus made it clear that a strong commitment to Him would produce every kind of suffering imaginable—even death. This has proven true throughout church history, in both oppressive and free societies, in dictatorships and democracies, among men and women, and in every corner of the world.

This is what separates the men from the boys in our walk with Jesus: being willing to suffer personal loss for the sake of Christ. Sadly, most men are merely afraid of what somebody else will think of them. They haven't faced a physical beating or career assassination because of their faith in Christ. Rather, somebody might look askance should they slip up and mention religion in public.

Personal suffering—the real kind that creates loss for a believer—prompts many Christian men to run for the hills. We have a heart for Jesus, but we have no backbone when the going gets rough.

When God's man fully identifies with Christ, things might get nasty. To keep us motivated, Jesus says, "Rejoice and be glad, because great is your reward in heaven" (Matthew 5:12).

Connect with the Word

Read Matthew 5:10-12.

1. What part does loyalty play in our walk with Christ?

2. Why did Jesus need to both warn followers and remind them of their reward?

3. Why do nonbelievers persecute believers? How should a Christian respond to suffering for Christ's sake?

4. Before you became a Christian, were you told to expect tough times? Did you think suffering was part of the call? If not, what did you expect?

5. What is the worst type of suffering for your faith that you could experience in the community where you live?

6. In the most practical terms, what does it mean to "rejoice and be glad" in the midst of persecution? What is your own experience of this?

Read 2 Timothy 1:6-12.

7. According to verse 6, what reminder do all believers need?

8. Where does courage to stand for Christ come from (verse 7)?

9. What two specific calls to action are found in verse 8? How have you tended to respond to these in the past?

10. According to verse 9, what should be the key motivating factor for God's man to stand his ground for Christ? How has this helped you stand so far?

11. In the end, why did Paul embrace suffering for Christ (verse 12)?

12. What impact does our stand for Christ—or our lack of commitment under pressure—have on other believers?

Connect with the Group

Group Opener
Discuss the group-opener question and the discussion questions that follow.

When was the last time you risked the disapproval of men to gain the approval of God? Tell the group what happened.

Discussion Questions

a. Why do so many men fear rejection for identifying fully with Christ? What should be our perspective on being rejected for our faith?

b. What doubts does suffering for believing in Christ create in some believers?

c. How does Jesus's own experience with suffering lend perspective to the issue?

d. What gives us boldness to take a stand for Christ? How can other men help God's man to stand? When have you seen this happen?

e. What personal habits give us strength when we're under pressure to cave in on our commitment to Christ? What works best for you?

f. How does suffering raise our relationship with God to a new level? What takes place relationally when suffering is involved in keeping a commitment? Talk about your own experience of this.

Standing Strong

In the space below, identify the situations or relationships in which you have difficulty standing for your faith. What would standing up for Christ look like in each case?

Ask the group to pray that God would give you boldness in your walk and new responses in the situations you've shared.

small-group resources

What if men aren't doing the Connect with the Word section before our small-group session?

Don't be discouraged. You set the pace. If you are doing the study and regularly referring to it in conversations with your men throughout the week, they will pick up on its importance. Here are some suggestions to motivate the men in your group to do their home Bible study:

- Send out a midweek e-mail in which you share your answer to one of the study questions. This shows them that you are personally committed to and involved in the study.

- Ask the guys to hit "respond to all" on their e-mail program and share one insight from that week's Bible study with the entire group. Encourage them to send it out before the next small-group session.

- Every time you meet, ask each man in the group to share one insight from his home study.

What if men are not showing up for small group?

This might mean they are losing a sin battle and don't want to admit it to the group. Or they might be consumed with other priorities. Or maybe they don't think they're getting anything out of the group. Here are some suggestions for getting the guys back each week:

- Affirm them when they show up, and tell them how much it means to you that they make small group a priority.

- From time to time, ask them to share one reason small group is important to them.
- Regularly call or send out an e-mail the day before you meet to remind them you're looking forward to seeing them.
- Check in with any guy who has missed more than one session and find out what's going on in his life.
- Get some feedback from the men. You may need to adjust your style. Listen and learn.

What if group discussion is not happening?

You are a discussion facilitator. You have to keep guys involved in the discussion or you'll lose them. You can engage a man who isn't sharing by saying, "Chuck, you've been quiet. What do you think about this question or discussion?" You should also be prepared to share your own personal stories that are related to the discussion questions. You'll set the example by the kind of sharing you do.

What if one man is dominating the group time?

You have to deal with it. If you don't, men will stop showing up. No one wants to hear from just one guy all the time. It will quickly kill morale. Meet with the guy in person and privately. Firmly but gently suggest that he allow others more time to talk. Be positive and encouraging, but truthful. You might say, "Bob, I notice how enthusiastic you are about the group and how you're always prepared to share your thoughts with the group. But there are some pretty quiet guys in the group too. Have you noticed? Would you be willing to help me get them involved in speaking up?"

How do I get the guys in my group more involved?

Give them something to do. Ask one guy to bring a snack. Invite another to lead the prayer time (ask in advance). Have a guy sub for you one week as the leader. (Meet with him beforehand to walk through the group program and the time allotments for each segment.) Encourage another guy to lead a subgroup.

What if guys are not being vulnerable during the Standing Strong or prayer times?

You model openness. You set the pace. Honesty breeds honesty. Vulnerability breeds vulnerability. Are you being vulnerable and honest about your own problems and struggles? (This doesn't mean that you have to spill your guts each week or reveal every secret of your life.) Remember, men want an honest, on-their-level leader who strives to walk with God. (Also, as the leader, you need an accountability partner, perhaps another group leader.)

What will we do at the first session?

We encourage you to open by discussing the **Small-Group Covenant** we've included in this resource section. Ask the men to commit to the study, and then discuss how long it will take your group to complete each session. (We suggest 75-90 minute sessions.) Men find it harder to come up with excuses for missing a group session if they have made a covenant to the other men right at the start.

Begin to identify ways certain men can play a more active role in small group. Give away responsibility. You won't feel as burdened, and your men will grow from the experience. Keep in mind that this process can take a few weeks. Challenge men to fulfill one of the group roles identified later in this resource section. If no one steps forward to fill a role, say to one of the men, "George, I've noticed that you are comfortable praying in a group. Would you lead us each week during that time?"

How can we keep the group connected after we finish a study?
Begin talking about starting another Bible study before you finish this eight-week study. (There are several other studies to choose from in the Every Man Bible study series.) Consider having a social time at the conclusion of the study, and encourage the men to invite a friend. This will help create momentum and encourage growth as you launch into another study with your group. There are probably many men in your church or neighborhood who aren't in small groups but would like to be. Be the kind of group that includes others.

As your group grows, consider choosing an apprentice leader who can take half the group into another room for the **Connect with the Group** time. That subgroup can stay together for prayer, or you can reconvene as a large group during that time. You could also meet for discussion as a large group and then break into subgroups for **Standing Strong** and **prayer.**

If your group doubles in size, it might be a perfect opportunity to release your apprentice leader with half the group to start another group. Allow men to pray about this and make a decision as a group. Typically, the relational complexities that come into play when a small group births a new group work themselves out. Allow guys to choose which group they'd like to be a part of. If guys are slow in choosing one group or another, ask them individually to select one of the groups. Take the lead in making this happen.

Look for opportunities for your group to serve in the church or community. Consider a local outreach project or a short-term missions trip. There are literally hundreds of practical ways you can serve the Lord in outreach. Check with your church leaders to learn the needs in your congregation or community. Create some interest by sending out scouts who will return with a report for the group. Serving keeps men from becoming self-focused and ingrown. When you serve as a group, you will grow as a group.

using this study in a large-group format

Many church leaders are looking for biblically based curriculum that can be used in a large-group setting, such as a Sunday-school class, or for small groups within an existing larger men's group. Each of the Every Man Bible studies can be adapted for this purpose. In addition, this curriculum can become a catalyst for churches wishing to launch men's small groups or to build a men's ministry.

Getting Started

Begin by getting the word out to men in your church, inviting them to join you for a men's study based on one of the topics in the Every Man Bible study series. You can place a notice in your church bulletin, have the pastor announce it from the pulpit, or pursue some other means of attracting interest.

Orientation Week

Arrange your room with round tables and chairs. Put approximately six chairs at each table.

Start your session in prayer and introduce your topic with a short but motivational message from any of the scriptures used in the Bible study. Hand out the curriculum and challenge the men to do their homework before each session. During this first session give the men some discussion questions based upon an overview of the material and have them talk things through within their small group around the table.

Just before you wrap things up, have each group select a table host or leader. You can do this by having everyone point at once to the person at their table they feel would best facilitate discussion for future meetings.

Ask those newly elected table leaders to stay after for a few minutes, and offer them an opportunity to be further trained as small-group leaders as they lead discussions throughout the course of the study.

Subsequent Weeks

Begin in prayer. Then give a short message (15-25 minutes) based upon the scripture used for that lesson. Pull out the most motivating topics or points, and strive to make the discussion relevant to the everyday life and world of a typical man. Then leave time for each table to work through the discussion questions listed in the curriculum. Be sure the discussion facilitators at each table close in prayer.

At the end of the eight sessions, you might want to challenge each "table group" to become a small group, inviting them to meet regularly with their new small-group leader and continue building the relationships they've begun.

prayer request record

Date:
Name:
Prayer Request:
Praise:

Date:
Name:
Prayer Request:
Praise:

Date:
Name:
Prayer Request:
Praise:

Date:
Name:
Prayer Request:
Praise:

Date:
Name:
Prayer Request:
Praise:

defining group roles

Group Leader: Leads the lesson and facilitates group discussion.

Apprentice Leader: Assists the leader as needed, which may include leading the lesson.

Refreshment Coordinator: Maintains a list of who will provide refreshments. Calls group members on the list to remind them to bring what they signed up for.

Prayer Warrior: Serves as the contact person for prayer between sessions. Establishes a list of those willing to pray for needs that arise. Maintains the prayer-chain list and activates the chain as needed by calling the first person on the list.

Social Chairman: Plans any desired social events during group sessions or at another scheduled time. Gathers members for planning committees as needed.

small-group roster

Name:
Address:
Phone: E-mail:

Name:
Address:
Phone: E-mail:

Name:
Address:
Phone: E-mail:

Name:
Address:
Phone: E-mail:

Name:
Address:
Phone: E-mail:

Name:
Address:
Phone: E-mail:

spiritual checkup

Your answers to the statements below will help you determine which areas you need to work on in order to grow spiritually. Mark the appropriate letter to the left of each statement. Then make a plan to take one step toward further growth in each area. Don't forget to pray for the Lord's wisdom before you begin. Be honest. Don't be overly critical or rationalize your weaknesses.

Y = Yes
S = Somewhat or Sometimes
N = No

My Spiritual Connection with Other Believers

____ I am developing relationships with Christian friends.
____ I have joined a small group.
____ I am dealing with conflict in a biblical manner.
____ I have become more loving and forgiving than I was a year ago.
____ I am a loving and devoted husband and father.

My Spiritual Growth

____ I have committed to daily Bible reading and prayer.
____ I am journaling on a regular basis, recording my spiritual growth.

____ I am growing spiritually by studying the Bible with others.

____ I am honoring God in my finances and personal giving.

____ I am filled with joy and gratitude for my life, even during trials.

____ I respond to challenges with peace and faith instead of anxiety and anger.

____ I avoid addictive behaviors (excessive drinking, overeating, watching too much TV, etc.).

Serving Christ and Others

____ I am in the process of discovering my spiritual gifts and talents.

____ I am involved in ministry in my church.

____ I have taken on a role or responsibility in my small group.

____ I am committed to helping someone else grow in his spiritual walk.

Sharing Christ with Others

____ I care about and am praying for those around me who are unbelievers.

____ I share my experience of coming to know Christ with others.

____ I invite others to join me in this group or for weekend worship services.

____ I am praying for others to come to Christ and am seeing this happen.

____ I do what I can to show kindness to people who don't know Christ.

Surrendering My Life for Growth

____ I attend church services weekly.

____ I pray for others to know Christ, and I seek to fulfill the Great Commission.

____ I regularly worship God through prayer, praise, and music, both at church and at home.

____ I care for my body through exercise, nutrition, and rest.

____ I am concerned about using my energy to serve God's purposes instead of my own.

My Identity in the Lord

____ I see myself as a beloved son of God, one whom God loves regardless of my sin.

____ I can come to God in all of my humanity and know that He accepts me completely. When I fail, I willingly run to God for forgiveness.

____ I experience Jesus as an encouraging Friend and Lord each moment of the day.

____ I have an abiding sense that God is on my side. I am aware of His gracious presence with me throughout the day.

____ During moments of beauty, grace, and human connection, I lift up praise and thanks to God.

____ I believe that using my talents to their fullest pleases the Lord.

____ I experience God's love for me in powerful ways.

small-group covenant

As a committed group member, I agree to the following:*

- **Regular Attendance.** I will attend group sessions on time and let everyone know in advance if I can't make it.
- **Group Safety.** I will help create a safe, encouraging environment where men can share their thoughts and feelings without fear of embarrassment or rejection. I will not judge other guys or attempt to fix their problems.
- **Confidentiality.** I will always keep to myself everything that is shared in the group.
- **Acceptance.** I will respect different opinions or beliefs and let Scripture be the teacher.
- **Accountability.** I will make myself accountable to the other group members for the personal goals I share.
- **Friendliness.** I will look for those around me who might join the group and explore their faith with other men.
- **Ownership.** I will prayerfully consider taking on a specific role within the group as the opportunity arises.
- **Spiritual Growth.** I will commit to establishing a daily quiet time with God, which includes doing the homework for this study. I will share with the group the progress I make and the struggles I experience as I seek to grow spiritually.

Signed: _____ Date: _____

---

* *Permission is given to photocopy and distribute this form to each man in your group. Review this covenant quarterly or as needed.*

about the authors

STEPHEN ARTERBURN is coauthor of the best-selling Every Man series. He is also founder and chairman of New Life Clinics, host of the daily *New Life Live!* national radio program, and creator of the Women of Faith conferences. A nationally known speaker and licensed minister, Stephen has authored more than forty books. He lives with his family in Laguna Beach, California.

KENNY LUCK is president and founder of Every Man Ministries, coauthor of *Every Man, God's Man* and its companion workbook, and coauthor of the Every Man Bible studies. He is the area leader for men's ministry and teaches a men's interactive Bible study at Saddleback Church in Lake Forest, California. He and his wife, Chrissy, have three children and reside in Trabuco Canyon, California.

TODD WENDORFF is a graduate of University of California, Berkeley, and holds a ThM from Talbot School of Theology. He serves as a teaching pastor at King's Harbor Church in Redondo Beach and is an adjunct professor at Biola University. He is an author of the Doing Life Together Bible study series. Todd and his wife, Denise, live with their three children in Rolling Hills Estates, California.

start a bible study
and connect with others
who want to be God's man.

Every Man Bible Studies are designed to help you discover, own,
and build on convictions grounded in God's word.